Facts About Countries
Bangladesh

Michael March

SEA-TO-SEA
Mankato Collingwood London

This edition first published in 2009 by
Sea-to-Sea Publications
Distributed by Black Rabbit Books
P.O. Box 3263
Mankato, Minnesota 56002

Library of Congress Cataloging-in-Publication Data:

March, Michael.
  Bangladesh / Michael March.
    p. cm. -- (Facts about countries)
  Includes index.
  Summary: "Describes the geography, history, industries, education,
government, and cultures of Bangladesh. Includes maps, charts, and
graphs"--Provided by publisher.
  ISBN 978-1-59771-113-5
  1. Bangladesh--Juvenile literature. I. Title.
  DS393.4.M353 2009
  954.92--dc22
                                                    2008004632

9 8 7 6 5 4 3 2

Published by arrangement with the Watts Publishing
Group Ltd, London.

Facts About Countries is produced for Franklin
Watts by Bender Richardson White, PO Box 266,
Uxbridge, UK.
Editor: Lionel Bender
Designer and Page Make-up: Ben White
Picture Researcher: Cathy Stastny
Cover Make-up: Mike Pilley, Radius
Production: Kim Richardson

Graphics and Maps: Stefan Chabluk
Educational Advisor: Prue Goodwin, Institute of
Education, The University of Reading
Consultant: Dr. Terry Jennings, a former geography
teacher and university lecturer. He is now a full-time
writer of children's geography and science books.

Picture Credits

Pages 1: Corbis Images/Roger Wood. 3: James Davis
Travel Photography. 4: Robert Harding/Liba Taylor.
7: Hutchison/Liba Taylor. 8: Hutchison/Dirk. R. Frans.
9, 11: Hutchison/Liba Taylor. 12-13: James Davis Travel
Photography. 14: Hutchison/Dirk R. Frans. 15: James
Davis Travel Photography. 17 top: Hutchison/Dirk R.
Frans. 17 bottom: Hutchison/Liba Taylor. 18: Robert
Harding Photo Library. 19: Hutchison/Liba Taylor.
20: Panos Pictures/Zed Nelson. 21: Hutchison Library.
22-23: Robert Harding/Liba Taylor. 23: Hutchison/
Trevor Page. 24: Hutchison/Bruce Wills. 25: Corbis
Images/Roger Wood. 26-27: James Davis Travel
Photography. 28: Robert Harding/Nigel Cromm.
30: Hutchison/Dirk R. Frans. 31: Hutchison Library.
Cover Photo: Eye Ubiquitous.

The Author

Michael March is a full-time writer and editor of non-fiction books. He has written more than 20 books for children about different countries of the world.

Note to parents and teachers

Every effort has been made by the Publishers to ensure that the websites in this book are suitable for children, that they are of the highest educational value, and that they contain no inappropriate or offensive material. However, because of the nature of the Internet, it is impossible to guarantee that the contents of these sites will not be altered. We strongly advise that Internet access is supervised by a responsible adult.

Contents

Welcome to Bangladesh

Bangladesh is a country in southern Asia. The land is mostly flat and often gets flooded.

Land of the Bengali people

The Bengalis are an ancient people, with a history going back thousands of years. Some 30 years ago, they set up their own independent country, Bangladesh. Before 1971, the region was part of Pakistan. Bangladeshis are famous for the handicrafts they produce, such as cotton clothes, embroidered silk robes, and delicate jewelry.

DATABASE

Neighbors

Bangladesh is surrounded by its huge neighbor, India. The coastline, to the south on the Bay of Bengal, is 360 miles (580km) long. To the southeast lies the country Burma (Myanmar).

Below. The capital city, Dhaka (which used to be spelled Dacca) is crowded, busy, and noisy.

4

NEPAL

BHUTAN

N
W E
S

Mountains   △ Mountain peak
Grassland and farming
☐ Capital   ○ Major city
Country boundary

0 ▭▭▭▭▭▭▭▭▭▭ 100 Miles
0 ▭▭▭▭▭▭▭▭▭▭ 100 Kilometers

26°N

● Rangpur

● Dinajpur

Bogra ●   Jamalpur ●   ● Sylhet   25°N

○ Mymensingh

Rajshahi ●

Ganges (Ganga) River

Brahmaputra (Jamuna) River

Kalni River

INDIA

Brahmanbaria ●   24°N

BANGLADESH

☐ DHAKA

Comilla ●

Tropic of
Cancer

Jessore ●

Haringhat River

Chandpur ●   23°N

CHITTAGONG HILLS

Khulna ●

Bagherhat ●   Barisal ●

Mongla Port ●

GANGES DELTA

Chittagong ●

Tahjindong △

S U N D A R B A N S

Sangu River   22°N

INDIA

Bay of Bengal

MYANMAR

88°E   89°E   90°E   91°E   92°E   21°N

The Land

Plants and Animals

Elephants and leopards live in the forests of the Chittagong Hills. The Sundarbans, in the southwest, is the world's largest mangrove forest. It is the home of the Bengal tiger. Altogether, Bangladesh has some 200 species of mammals, 120 species of reptiles, 700 species of birds, and 200 species of fish.

Much of Bangladesh is low-lying land around the Brahmaputra and Ganges rivers. Flooding from the rivers and the sea has created a very fertile soil.

Hill country

Only about one-tenth of Bangladesh is hilly. Most of the hills are in the southeast. Forests grow on some of the higher areas.

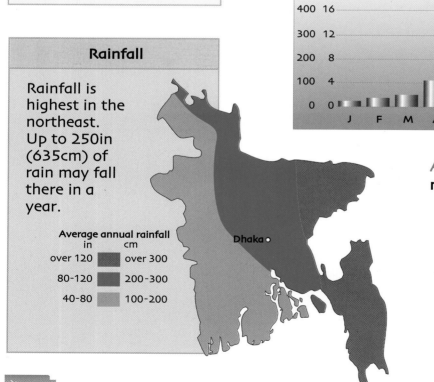

Above. **How much rain falls each month in Dhaka.**

Rainfall

Rainfall is highest in the northeast. Up to 250in (635cm) of rain may fall there in a year.

Average annual rainfall

in	cm
over 120	over 300
80-120	200-300
40-80	100-200

Dhaka

Climate

In Bangladesh it is warm, or hot and damp all year round. The east of the country gets about three times as much rain as the west. Most of the rain falls between May and September, during the monsoon, when one-third of the country becomes flooded. At other times, there are droughts.

Between April and October there are sometimes violent storms along the coast. In 1970, a storm killed about 500,000 people. In 1991 another storm cost 120,000 lives and left millions of people homeless.

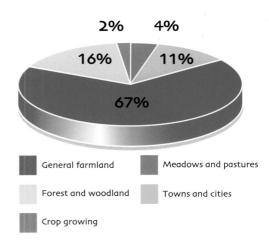

2%   4%

16%   11%

67%

■ General farmland ■ Meadows and pastures
■ Forest and woodland ■ Towns and cities
■ Crop growing

Above. **How land is used in Bangladesh.**

Below. **In the countryside, most houses have a thatched or corrugated iron roof.**

Web Search ▶▶

▶ www.bangladeshonline.
  com/bmd/
  Bangladesh's climate and weather.

▶ www.worldinfozone.com/
  country.php?country=
  Bangladesh
  Information on Bangladesh's climate, plants, and animals.

▶ www.discoverybangladesh.
  com/dream_dest_
  chittagong.html
  Tourist information about Chittagong.

The People

Bangladesh has about 133 million people. It is the world's seventh-largest country in terms of population.

A mix of peoples

Most Bengalis originally came from the regions that are today Burma (Myanmar), northern India, and Tibet in China. They mixed and bred with the local people of different races and religions.

Below. In the towns, the streets are crowded with rickshaws.

Above. **Native Bengalis often have dark skin and black hair. They are usually of medium height and build.**

Right. **Numbers of men and women in Bangladesh.**

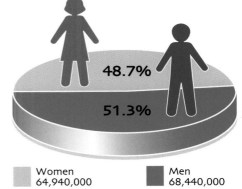

48.7%

51.3%

Women
64,940,000

Men
68,440,000

Age groups

Bangladesh is a young country. More than one-third of the population is under 15 years of age, and half under 25. Only about three percent of people are aged 65 or older.

Boys outnumber girls, and men outnumber women, in every age group. The biggest difference between numbers of men and women is in the over 65s, where there are about 10 percent more men than women. Overall, Bangladeshi men outnumber women by five percent. Fifty years ago, this difference was nearly 10 percent.

Web Search ▶▶

► www.discoverybangladesh.
   com/meetbangladesh/
   statistic.html
   Facts and figures about the
   population of Bangladesh.

► www.bbsgov.org/
   Bangladesh government's
   Bureau of Statistics.

Town and Country Life

Bangladesh is one of the most densely populated countries on Earth. There are 1,978 persons per square mile (920 per square km). The population is growing at a rate of between 1.5 and 2 percent a year.

Where people live

About 9 million people live in Dhaka. It is by far the biggest city. The Chittagong Hills and the Sundarbans, a region of swamps, have fewer people than other areas. Approximately three-quarters of the population live in the countryside but many people are now moving to the towns.

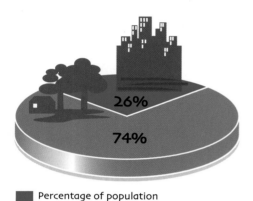

26%

74%

■ Percentage of population living in cities and towns

■ Percentage of population living in the countryside

Above. **Where people live.**

Clothing

Many Bangladeshi men wear the traditional *lungi,* a kind of skirt, and often go barefoot. Most women wear the traditional *saree,* a wide strip of cotton or silk that is wrapped around the body and draped over a shoulder.

Population

Most cities and towns are crowded with people and this is getting worse.

Persons per square mile	Persons per square km
Less than 2.5	Less than 1
2.5–250	1–100
250–500	100–200
500–1750	200–700
More than 1,750	More than 700

Dhaka

Houses and homes

In the countryside, villagers build small houses of bamboo, with one or two rooms for a family. Most houses have no electricity. In times of serious flooding, people move onto the roof or live in small boats.

In the towns and cities, some families have brick or concrete homes or live in small apartment buildings. But many live crowded together in small wooden houses.

Below. In the countryside, most people get their drinking water from wells.

Right. Almost everyone can get clean drinking water, but few homes have plumbing.

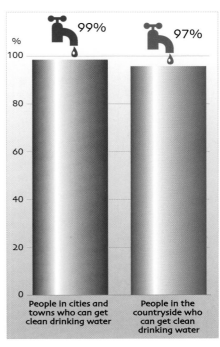

99%   97%

%		
100		
80		
60		
40		
20		
0	People in cities and towns who can get clean drinking water	People in the countryside who can get clean drinking water

Web Search ▶▶

▶ www.discoverybangladesh.com/meetbangladesh/demographic_feature.html
Website about where people live in Bangladesh.

▶ www.world-gazetteer.com/
Information on populations of cities, towns, and regions of Bangladesh.

▶ www.bangladeshonline.com/tourism/popu.htm
Facts and figures on visitors to and from Bangladesh.

Farming and Fishing

More than half the workers of Bangladesh work on the land. Most of them are rice farmers. Rice and fish are the main foods that people eat.

Main crops

Many of the 17 million farmers own small areas of land—about the size of three soccer fields. They farm using hand tools and animals such as bullocks. In areas where it is hot and wet, rice can be grown and harvested three times each year. The main crops grown for export are tea and jute. Jute is used to make rope and mats.

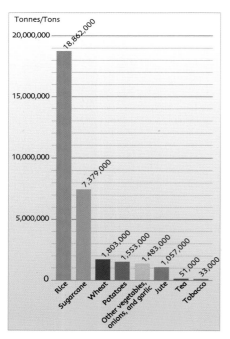

Above. **The different crops grown in Bangladesh.**

Farming Regions

The major areas for farming are in the south and west of the country.

○ Rice
🐄 Cattle
▦ Jute

▦ Pasture
▦ Forest

Dhaka ○

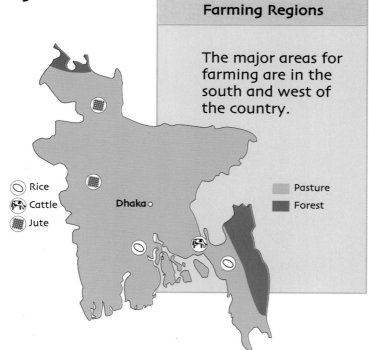

Fruit, leather, fish, and shellfish

Farmers also grow vegetables, sugarcane, and a wide variety of fruit, including mangoes and bananas. Cattle are kept mainly for the leather from their skins.

More than a million Bangladeshis fish for a living. Hilsa, a kind of herring, and shrimp are the main fish catch. Shrimp are also farmed in special ponds for export. Catfish, carp, and other species are fished in the country's many rivers.

Shift and Burn

Some Bangladeshis make land for farming by cutting down trees and burning them. They use the ashes as fertilizer. They then sow the seeds and harvest the crop, before moving onto another patch. The first patch is then left to return to grass or forest.

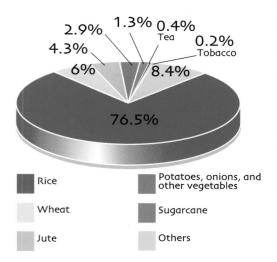

2.9% 1.3% 0.4%
Tea
4.3% 0.2%
Tobacco
6% 8.4%
76.5%

- Rice
- Wheat
- Jute
- Potatoes, onions, and other vegetables
- Sugarcane
- Others

Above. **Crops grown, by weight.**

Web Search ▶▶

▶ www.bbsgov.org/
Information on farm production.

▶ www.sdnbd.org/sdi/
metadata/bangladesh_
data_profile.htm
Sustainable Development Networking Project in Bangladesh.

▶ www.fao.org/fi/statist/
summtab/default.asp
United Nations' Food and Agriculture Organization website.

Left. **Fishermen unload their catch of freshwater fish on a riverbank in Dhaka.**

Resources and Industry

DATABASE

Cheap labor

Many factories produce clothing and knitwear, which are major exports. Other factories turn jute into burlap (for making sacks), or make leather goods and steel. Service industries include banking, hotels, transportation, and catering. Labor is cheap. Many workers are paid less than $1.50 a day.

About one-third of Bangladeshi workers work in factories, or in industries such as banking, transportation, and tourism, which are called service industries.

Energy supplies

Bangladesh has more than 20 gas fields, some of them offshore in the Bay of Bengal. Natural gas and coal provide 90 percent of the country's electricity. The rest comes from hydroelectric power from the country's rivers.

Below. **Sewing in a clothes factory.**

Right. **Output of manufactured goods.**

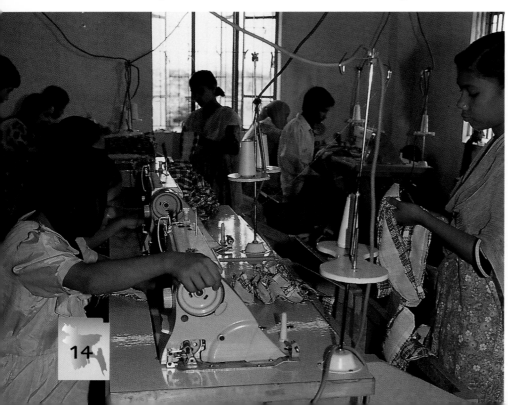

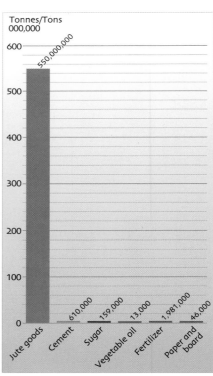

Tonnes/Tons
000,000

Jute goods	550,000,000
Cement	610,000
Sugar	159,000
Vegetable oil	13,000
Fertilizer	1,981,000
Paper and board	46,000

Using resources

Most of the fuel used in homes for heating and cooking comes from wood, animal dung, or crop waste. The rest comes from oil.

Natural gas is used to make fertilizer, a major export. Sand is used in glass-making. Limestone and hard rock provide cement and other materials used to make buildings. Bamboo is pulped to make paper.

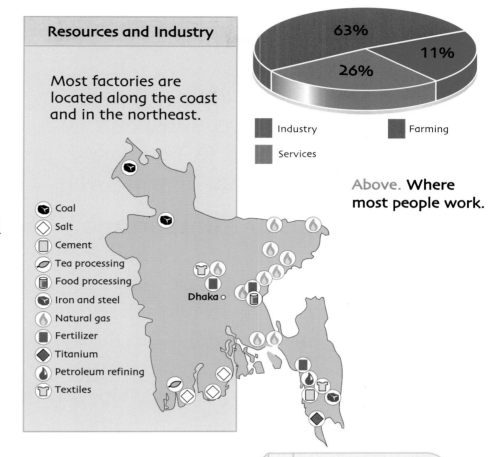

Resources and Industry

Most factories are located along the coast and in the northeast.

- ☸ Coal
- ◇ Salt
- ▢ Cement
- ⬮ Tea processing
- ▣ Food processing
- ☸ Iron and steel
- ◐ Natural gas
- ▪ Fertilizer
- ◆ Titanium
- ◑ Petroleum refining
- ⬒ Textiles

Dhaka ○

63% 11% 26%

■ Industry ■ Farming
■ Services

Above. **Where most people work.**

Below. **At a brickworks outside Dhaka, firewood is burned to heat ovens in which the bricks are baked.**

Web Search ▶▶

▶ www.virtualbangladesh.com/
economy/
Information about
Bangladeshi industry.

▶ www.bbsgov.org/
Government facts and figures
on industry.

▶ www.discoverybangladesh.
com/meetbangladesh/
economy.html
Website about energy and
industry.

Transportation

Biman, Bangladesh's airline, flies to different cities in the country and abroad. Most journeys in Bangladesh are made by road, railroad, or waterway.

Different forms of transportation

Bangladesh has cargo ships, container ships, and oil tankers. Most of the country's imports and exports go through the seaports of Chittagong and Mongla. More than 1,400 ships call at Chittagong harbor every year. Mongla handles more than 300 ships a year.

Inland, river ports are also important. During the monsoon season, there are 4,970 miles (8,000km) of waterways that can be used by boats. But during the dry season, this shrinks to 3,106 miles (5,000km).

Today, most passengers and goods in Bangladesh go by road. Bus services link all the main towns.

The railroads, which are owned by the state, run 300 locomotives, 1,200 passenger coaches, and 16,000 freight wagons between more than 500 stations.

Bicycles and Rickshaws

Of all journeys in Dhaka, 40 percent are made by bicycle. Dhaka has 600,000 bicycle rickshaws—colorfully decorated passenger vehicles that are based on a bicycle. These are used both by local people and by tourists. Autorickshaws are similar but motorized, and are therefore quicker.

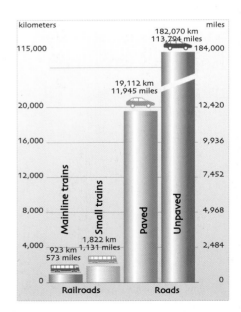

Above. **The lengths of the railroad and road systems.**

Transportation

All the transportation systems are centered on Dhaka, the captial city.

Dinajpur

Rangpur

Jamalpur

Bogra

Sylhet

Rajshahi

Dhaka

Narayang

Comilla

Jessore

Khulna

Barisal

Mongla Port

Chittagong

⊗ Major airport
— Main roads
∿ Railroads
∿ Main rivers

Above. Mainline trains, like this one in Dhaka, are larger than the trains used in the countryside.

Below. In the countryside, wooden rafts are used as ferryboats.

Web Search ▶▶

▶ www.bbsgov.org/
Government information about transportation.

▶ www.discoverybangladesh.com/transportation.html
Information about Bangladesh's transportation systems.

Education

In Bangladesh, children go to primary school from age six to 11. Many go on to secondary school until 16. A few stay at school until 18 and then enter university.

Primary and secondary schools

All children must go to primary school, which is free. Children study Bangla, English, math, and science. They are also taught skills to help their parents at home.

Secondary education is not generally free and many children do not attend. But the government pays for some girls to stay at school so they do not give up their studies to marry young. Schools called *madrasas* are religious. There, the religion of Islam is taught as well as other subjects.

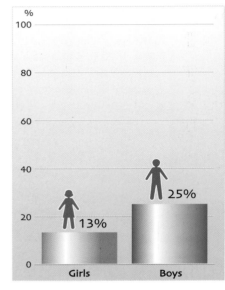

Above. **Percentages of boys and girls who go on to secondary education.**

Right. **A classroom in a village school.**

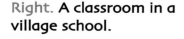

University education

Secondary schools in cities are the best equipped. Often, village schools have too few teachers and not many books.

Children who want to go to university or to a college of technology must pass the School and Higher School Certificate exams. The University of Dhaka is the largest in Bangladesh.

DATABASE

Numbers of Bangladeshis in education

Primary school
16.76 million
Secondary school
4.87 million
Colleges 1.57 million
University   129,500

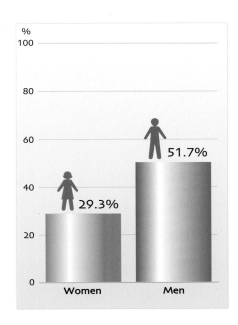

Above. **Bangladeshis who can read and write.**

Below. **Young women being taught how to embroider clothes.**

Web Search ▶▶

▶ www.unicef.org/infoby country/bangladesh_ bangladesh_contact.html
UNESCO International Bureau of Education survey.

▶ www.unicef.org/girls education/index.html
Type "girls' education" into the search engine to find UNESCO facts about girls' education worldwide.

Sports and Leisure

Among Bangladeshis, cricket, field hockey, and soccer are the most popular sports. Kabbadi is the national game.

Traditional sports

Kabbadi (see below) began as a way of developing self-defense skills among unarmed people. Another traditional sport is boat racing. Every year, on rivers and canals, teams of villagers race against each other in colorful rowboats.

Below. **Children practice their soccer skills watched by their teacher.**

DATABASE

Bangabandhu Stadium

International cricket has been played at the Dhaka stadium since 1955. In 1971, the stadium was renamed the Bangabandhu Stadium in honor of Bangabandhu Sheikh Mujibur-Rahman, who founded Bangladesh as an independent country.

Kabbadi

This traditional game is like "touch football" but without a ball. It lasts 40 minutes. "Raiders" go one at a time into their opponents' half of the court to touch the "enemy." The raider must return to his half without drawing another breath. If he succeeds, then the players he touches are "out." But if his enemy holds him so that he cannot get back before taking a breath, then it is the raider who is "out."

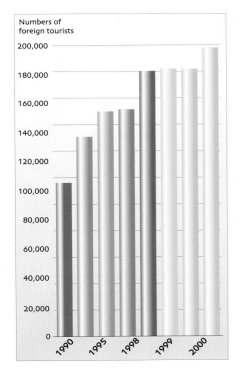

Numbers of
foreign tourists

Above. **Tourists visiting Bangladesh**

Above. **At a school sports gala, students perform a traditional martial arts display.**

A sporting nation

In 2000, Bangladesh was recognized in cricket as a test match side. The country also made history in chess by producing, in 1986, the first Grandmaster from the Indian subcontinent.

Some 30 National Sports Federations run cricket, field hockey, soccer, tennis, boxing, cycling, and basketball across the country. Women have separate sports federations.

Web Search ▶▶

▶ www.abyznewslinks.com/
bangl.htm
Information about sport in
Bangladeshi newspapers.

▶ www.aboutaball.co.uk/html2/
countries/bangladesh.php
Soccer in Bangladesh.

▶ www.gamecricket.com/asia-
cup-bangladesh-team.html
Cricket in Bangladesh.

21

Daily Life and Religion

The nation's health and welfare services are improving and people are living longer. But wages are low and electrical goods, such as televisions, are expensive.

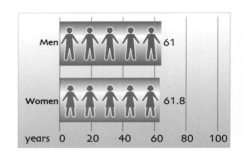

Above. The average age Bangladeshis can expect to live to.

Healthcare

Healthcare in Bangladesh is improving, with 70 percent of children now being protected against diseases such as polio and diphtheria, compared with just 55 percent 10 years ago.

Welfare services are now being developed to help pregnant women, disabled people, senior citizens, and the unemployed.

Religion

Most Bangladeshis are Muslims. They follow the religion of Islam. Each day, Muslims visit their local mosque to pray. A mosque is a Muslim house of worship.

Right. A street trader in Dhaka. Most people buy their food, clothes, and household goods from market stands and small retail outlets.

Poverty

More than one-third of the population of Bangladesh is poor. Most people there earn about $470.00 a year, so they cannot afford to buy luxuries such as a television set or a computer. To buy a used car would take more than 20 years' savings for a typical Bangladeshi.

Above. **A Buddhist temple in a village in Chittagong.**

Right. **Followers of the main religions.**

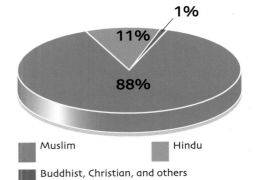

1%
11%
88%

■ Muslim   ■ Hindu
■ Buddhist, Christian, and others

The Working Week

Retailers and offices open between 9 A.M. and 5 P.M., Saturday to Friday. Sunday is a normal working day, and Friday is a day off for Muslim worship.

Web Search ▶▶

▶ www.citechco.net/bangla desh/religion.html
Information about religion in Bangladesh.

Arts and Media

Bangladesh is well known for its art, architecture, dance, drama, and music.

Old and new

The most beautiful buildings in the country are mosques and temples that are hundreds of years old. They are covered with carvings and decorations. Bengali artists usually paint scenes of everyday life. The most famous paintings are by Zainul Abedin. Bengali writer Rabindranath Tagore (1861-1941) won the Nobel Prize for Literature in 1913.

DATABASE

The movies

The first full-length Bangladeshi motion picture was made in 1956. Today, the country makes about 60 movies a year. *The Clay Bird*, released in 2003, was very popular. It tells the story of a boy growing up in Bangladesh in the 1960s during the time when it was struggling for independence.

Below. **Posters for a Bangladeshi movie at a theater in Dhaka.**

24

Singing

Traditional folksongs in the styles called *jari* and *shari* are sung while instruments such as the *banshi* (bamboo flute) and *eklara* (a single-stringed lute) are played. Men and women perform a dance to the music.

The media

About 200 daily newspapers are published in Bangladesh. Some 37 percent of people have access to a radio, but only about 10 percent to a TV. Radio and TV stations are run by the government, but there are also commercial and satellite stations.

Above. **A woman performs a traditional dance.**

Below. **Television and radio broadcast stations.**

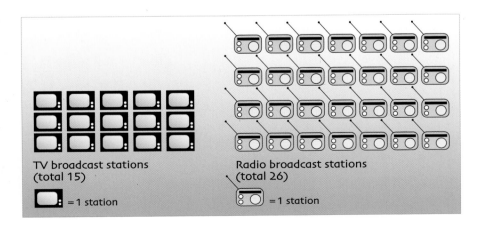

TV broadcast stations (total 15)

= 1 station

Radio broadcast stations (total 26)

= 1 station

Web Search ►►

► www.comminit.com/
strategicthinking/st2002/
thinking-386.html
Bangladeshi radio.

► www.discoverybangladesh.
com/meetbangladesh/art.
html
Information about writers, art, music, dance, and drama in Bangladesh.

Government

Tax

The government raises taxes to pay for healthcare, transportation, housing, and so on. Most of the tax comes from customs duties on imported goods. People earning 225,000 takas ($4,720) or more a year pay between 10 and 25 percent in income tax.

Bangladesh is governed by elected members of Parliament, headed by a prime minister. The president is the official head of state.

President and government

The president and parliament serve for up to five years. There are 300 members of parliament, each of whom is elected by the people of his or her own area. Voting is open to Bangladeshi citizens from the age

Provinces and Districts

The country is divided into six main administrative areas, called divisions or provinces. These are further divided into districts.

Right. The Parliament building in Dhaka, the capital city.

of 18. There are several political parties. The party that gains the most seats in the election forms the government. That party's leader, with the president's approval, becomes the prime minister.

Religion and free speech

The state religion of Bangladesh is Islam but Muslims are not favored in any way over followers of other religions. Laws and regulations also state that men and women must be treated equally, that there should be a free press, and that everyone should be allowed freedom of speech.

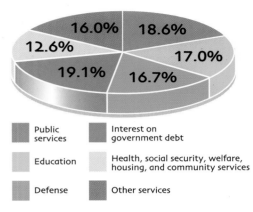

16.0% 18.6%
12.6%
19.1% 16.7% 17.0%

Public services	Interest on government debt
Education	Health, social security, welfare, housing, and community services
Defense	Other services

Above. **How the government spends its money and the interest it pays on money borrowed from other countries.**

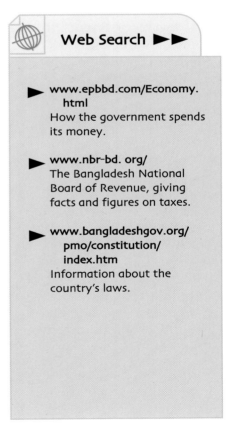

Web Search ▶▶

▶ www.epbbd.com/Economy. html
How the government spends its money.

▶ www.nbr-bd. org/
The Bangladesh National Board of Revenue, giving facts and figures on taxes.

▶ www.bangladeshgov.org/ pmo/constitution/ index.htm
Information about the country's laws.

Place in the World

DATABASE

Important dates to 1974

500 B.C.E. Tribal people establish kingdom of Vanga (Bengal)

C.E. 750–1200 Rule by Buddhist and Hindu leaders

1576 Conquered by Muslim Mughul emperor Akbar

1757 British become the new rulers of the Indian subcontinent

1947 British leave and divide subcontinent into India (Hindu) and Pakistan (Muslim). East Bengal becomes part of Pakistan, but with India in between the two parts

1971 Bengali nationalists proclaim independent republic of Bangladesh, and civil war follows. West Pakistan armies defeated with help from India

1972 First government of People's Republic of Bangladesh, with Sheikh Mujibur-Rahman as prime minister

The People's Republic of Bangladesh began in war and revolution in 1971.

Independence and beyond

In 1947, when the British finally left their main colonies in Asia, the region was split in two: India was to be mainly for Hindus, and Pakistan for Muslims. But there were two parts to Pakistan, separated by 932 miles (1,500km): West Pakistan and East Pakistan, which was in Bengal.

Below. **The High Court in Dhaka, center of the legal system.**

In 1971, East Pakistan tried to become independent and known as Bangladesh. It was attacked by the army of West Pakistan. About three million people were killed before Bangladesh won independence in 1972.

In 1974, it joined the United Nations (UN). Bangladesh also belongs to the British Commonwealth.

Over the last 10 years, Bangladesh's wealth has doubled. By 2010, the country aims to halve the number of its poor people, which stands at about 45 million. To do this, its economy must grow by 48 percent. This is a big challenge.

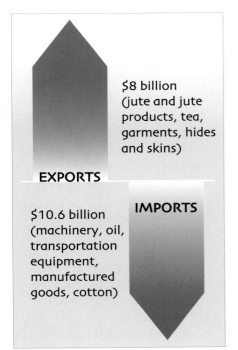

$8 billion (jute and jute products, tea, garments, hides and skins)

EXPORTS

$10.6 billion (machinery, oil, transportation equipment, manufactured goods, cotton)

IMPORTS

Left. The value of Bangladesh's exports and imports.

Web Search ▶▶

▶ www.geographyiq.com/countries/bg/Bangladesh_history_summary.htm
History of the Bangladesh region.

▶ www.worldbank.org/bd
World Bank website about Bangladesh.

▶ www.un-bd.org/
The United Nations in Bangladesh.

DATABASE

Important dates since 1974

1974 Bangladesh takes its seat at the UN

1975 Sheikh Mujib assassinated in military takeover. Four years of martial law follow

1981 President Zia Rahman, founder of the Bangladesh National Party (BNP), is assassinated

1986 Parliamentary elections won by Jatiya (People's) Party (JP)

1988 Islam made the state religion. Flooding kills thousands of people and leaves 30 million homeless

1991–96 BNP, led by widow of Zia Rahman, heads government after new elections

1996 BNP re-elected, but Awami League (AL), led by Sheikh Mujib's daughter, forms new government after fresh elections

2001 BNP re-elected after period of strikes

Area:
56977 sq miles
(147,570 sq km)

Population size:
133.4 million

Capital city:
Dhaka (population 8,942,300)

Other major cities:
Chittagong (2,592,400),
Khulna (1,211,500),
Rajshahi (712,400), Gazipur
(520,800), Narayaganj
(357,300)

Longest river:
Ganges–Padma (part of
Ganges) (190 miles/306 km)

Highest mountain:
Tahjindong (4,632ft/1,412 m)

Currency:
Taka (Tk)

Flag:
The red disk represents the
sun of freedom and the
blood that was shed to
achieve independence. The
green background represents
the Bangladeshi countryside
and is the traditional color
of Islam.

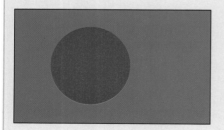

Languages:
Official language: Bangla
(Bengali)

Natural resources
Natural gas, coal, lignite,
peat, a little oil, limestone,
sand, ceramic clay, hard
rock, jute, bamboo

Major exports:
Ready-made clothes, jute
and jute goods, tea, leather
and leather goods, newsprint
(paper for newspapers), fish,
frozen foods

Some holidays and festivals
January 1: New Year's Day.
Early March (11th lunar
 month): Pawhela Falgun,
 "First Day of Spring" when
 people attend fairs,
 exchange greetings,
 flowers, cards, and gifts.

March 26: Independence
 Day. Anniversary of the
 declaration of
 independence from
 Pakistan in 1971.
Mid-April (1st day, 1st
 lunar month): Pawhela
 Boishakh (Bengali New
 Year). Singing and fairs
 to mark the beginning of
 the Bengali New Year.
August 15: Anniversary of
 the assassination, in
 1975, of Sheikh Mujibur-
 Rahman, the father
 of the Bangladesh nation.

Official religion:
Islam

Other religions
Hindu 11 percent,
Buddhist and Christian
0.9 percent,
Others 0.1 percent

Key Words

BUDDHISM
Religion based on the teachings of Siddhartha Gautama, also known as the Buddha, who was born in India in 563 B.C.E.

COMMONWEALTH (OF NATIONS)
Association of independent countries, nearly all of which once belonged to the British Empire.

CROPS
Plants grown for food or for products to sell, such as cotton and jute.

DROUGHT
A long period without rain.

ECONOMY
The business of money, industry, and resources.

EXPORTS
Goods or products sold to other countries.

FLOOD
When a river bursts its banks or the sea is blown inland and water covers flat land.

HINDUISM
A 4,000-year-old religion that began in India, and is the major religion of India.

HYDROELECTRIC POWER
Electrical power created from flowing water, such as a river that has been dammed to provide energy for an electricity generator in a power station.

IMPORTS
Goods or products bought in from other countries.

INDEPENDENT
Ruled by people living in the country and not by another country.

ISLAM
Religion begun by Muhammad, the Prophet, in C.E. 622 in what is today Saudi Arabia.

JUTE
A woody herb and its fibers, grown in river valleys and used to make string, matting, carpets, sacking, and other products.

MANGROVES
Leafy tropical trees that grow in shallow, salty water near the coast.

MONSOON
A wind that brings moisture from the sea and deposits it on the land as rain in the summer months.

REPUBLIC
A country whose leaders are elected to govern, rather than, for example, rule by a king or queen, when the power of leadership is handed down through generations.

RESOURCES
A country's supplies of energy, natural materials, and minerals.

RICKSHAW
A passenger vehicle powered by bicycle or motor scooter.

SUBCONTINENT
A large land mass, made up of several countries, such as India, Pakistan, and Bangladesh, but smaller than the whole continent.

Index